SELF-PORTRAIT

IN A

CONVEX MIRROR

Praise for
Self-Portrait in a Convex Mirror

"Poems of breathtaking freshness and adventure in which dazzling orchestrations of language open up whole areas of consciousness no other American poet has ever begun to explore."

—John Malcolm Brinnin, *The New York Times*

"Ashbery is astonishingly original, and though his mannerisms have been widely imitated, he himself has imitated no one. . . . Because Ashbery acknowledges that our being-in-time is bearable, because he has rejected the theatrics of the long lament, because he renders honestly the cheerful, amateurish way we make do, for these reasons his poetry is all the more deserving of our trust and respect—and all the more harrowing."

—Edmund White

"The title poem may well be the most intelligent thing of its kind ever written: the one which best combines, in other words, an authentic poetic impulse with an understanding of what painting is all about."

—John Russell, *The New York Times*

"He is a poet of genius."   —*The Guardian*

"The sheer range of Ashbery's style is unparalleled among contemporary writers."   —Fred Moramarco, *The American Poetry Review*

"*Self-Portrait in a Convex Mirror* is certainly one of the most sustained performances in American writing. . . . John Ashbery, more than any other contemporary, is the poet of the momentary, the transitory. This preoccupation animates everything he writes, and what he writes is some of the best poetry of our day."

—Edmund Keeley, *The Washington Post*

"Mr. Ashbery belongs to everyone interested in poetry or modern art, or just the possibility of change. He is the great original of his generation."

—David Bromwich, *The Georgia Review*

"A style devoid of pretension and a beautiful ease of manner that is rarely less than enchanting . . . There is no one who writes quite like Ashbery, and the poetic territory he inhabits is very much his own."

—Paul Auster

SELF-PORTRAIT IN A CONVEX MIRROR

John Ashbery was born in Rochester, New York, in 1927. He earned degrees from Harvard and Columbia and went to France as a Fulbright Scholar in 1955, living there for much of the next decade. His many collections of poetry include *Planisphere* (2009) and *Notes from the Air: Selected Later Poems* (2007), which was awarded the 2008 International Griffin Poetry Prize; an early book, *Some Trees*, was selected by W. H. Auden for the Yale Younger Poets Series (1956), and in 2008 the Library of America published the first volume of his collected poems. He has published numerous translations from the French, including works by Pierre Reverdy, Arthur Rimbaud, Raymond Roussel, and several collections of poems by Pierre Martory. Also active in other areas of the arts, he has served as executive editor of *Art News*, and as art critic for *New York* magazine and *Newsweek*; the first solo exhibition of his collages was held at the Tibor de Nagy Gallery (New York) in 2008. He taught for many years at Brooklyn College and Bard College, and in 1989–90 delivered the Charles Eliot Norton lectures at Harvard. He is a member of the American Academy of Arts and Letters and the American Academy of Arts and Sciences, and was a Chancellor of the Academy of American Poets from 1988 to 1999. The winner of many prizes and awards, both nationally and internationally, he has received two Guggenheim Fellowships and was a MacArthur Fellow from 1985 to 1990. His work has been translated into more than twenty-five languages. He lives in New York. Additional information is available in the "About John Ashbery" section of the Ashbery Resource Center's Web site, a project of The Flow Chart Foundation, www.flowchartfoundation.org/arc.

Also by John Ashbery

POETRY
Turandot and Other Poems
Some Trees
The Tennis Court Oath
Rivers and Mountains
The Double Dream of Spring
Three Poems
The Vermont Notebook
Self-Portrait in a Convex Mirror
Houseboat Days
As We Know
Shadow Train
A Wave
Selected Poems
April Galleons
Flow Chart
Hotel Lautréamont
And the Stars Were Shining
Can You Hear, Bird
Wakefulness
The Mooring of Starting Out
Girls on the Run
Your Name Here
As Umbrellas Follow Rain
Chinese Whispers
Where Shall I Wander
A Worldly Country
Notes from the Air: Selected Later Poems
Collected Poems 1956–1987
Planisphere
Quick Question

FICTION
A Nest of Ninnies [*with James Schuyler*]

PLAYS
Three Plays

CRITICISM AND ESSAYS
Reported Sightings: Art Chronicles 1957–1987
Other Traditions [*The Charles Eliot Norton Lectures*]
Selected Prose

SELF-PORTRAIT

IN A

CONVEX MIRROR

POEMS BY

John Ashbery

PENGUIN BOOKS

PENGUIN BOOKS
Published by the Penguin Group
Penguin Group (USA) Inc., 375 Hudson Street, New York, New York 10014, U.S.A.
Penguin Group (Canada), 90 Eglinton Avenue East, Suite 700, Toronto, Ontario, Canada M4P 2Y3
(a division of Pearson Penguin Canada Inc.)
Penguin Books Ltd, 80 Strand, London WC2R 0RL, England
Penguin Ireland, 25 St Stephen's Green, Dublin 2, Ireland (a division of Penguin Books Ltd)
Penguin Group (Australia), 250 Camberwell Road, Camberwell, Victoria 3124, Australia
(a division of Pearson Australia Group Pty Ltd)
Penguin Books India Pvt Ltd, 11 Community Centre, Panchsheel Park, New Delhi – 110 017, India
Penguin Group (NZ), 67 Apollo Drive, Rosedale, North Shore 0632, New Zealand
(a division of Pearson New Zealand Ltd)
Penguin Books (South Africa) (Pty) Ltd, 24 Sturdee Avenue, Rosebank, Johannesburg 2196,
South Africa

Penguin Books Ltd, Registered Offices:
80 Strand, London WC2R 0RL, England

First published by The Viking Press 1975
Published in Penguin Books 1976

35 37 39 40 38 36

Copyright © John Ashbery, 1972, 1973, 1974, 1975
All rights reserved

Text redesigned, in collaboration with the author, in 2009.

LIBRARY OF CONGRESS CATALOGING IN PUBLICATION DATA
Ashbery, John
Self-portrait in a convex mirror.
(The Penguin poets)
I. Title.
[ps3501.s475s4 1976]   811' .5' 4   76-18814
ISBN 978-0-14-058668-8

Printed in the United States of America
Set in Adobe Garamond

"Voyage in the Blue," "Fear of Death," "City Afternoon," and "Worsening Situation" originally appeared in *The New Yorker*. "Scheherazade," "As You Came from the Holy Land," "A Man of Words," "Grand Galop," and "Self-Portrait in a Convex Mirror" originally appeared in *Poetry*.

Other poems have appeared in *American Poetry Review, American Review, The New York Review of Books*, and in various little magazines.

I wish to thank the Guggenheim Foundation for a grant which was of great help in writing this book.
—*J. A.*

for David Kermani

CONTENTS

SELF-PORTRAIT

IN A

CONVEX MIRROR

On the following pages, a stanza break occurs at the bottom of the page (not including pages in which the break is evident because of the regular stanzaic structure of the poem): 6, 22, 33, 36, 69.

As One Put Drunk into the Packet-Boat

I tried each thing, only some were immortal and free.
Elsewhere we are as sitting in a place where sunlight
Filters down, a little at a time,
Waiting for someone to come. Harsh words are spoken,
As the sun yellows the green of the maple tree....

So this was all, but obscurely
I felt the stirrings of new breath in the pages
Which all winter long had smelled like an old catalogue.
New sentences were starting up. But the summer
Was well along, not yet past the mid-point
But full and dark with the promise of that fullness,
That time when one can no longer wander away
And even the least attentive fall silent
To watch the thing that is prepared to happen.

A look of glass stops you
And you walk on shaken: was I the perceived?
Did they notice me, this time, as I am,
Or is it postponed again? The children
Still at their games, clouds that arise with a swift
Impatience in the afternoon sky, then dissipate
As limpid, dense twilight comes.
Only in that tooting of a horn
Down there, for a moment, I thought
The great, formal affair was beginning, orchestrated,
Its colors concentrated in a glance, a ballade
That takes in the whole world, now, but lightly,
Still lightly, but with wide authority and tact.

The prevalence of those gray flakes falling?
They are sun motes. You have slept in the sun

Longer than the sphinx, and are none the wiser for it.
Come in. And I thought a shadow fell across the door
But it was only her come to ask once more
If I was coming in, and not to hurry in case I wasn't.

The night sheen takes over. A moon of cistercian pallor
Has climbed to the center of heaven, installed,
Finally involved with the business of darkness.
And a sigh heaves from all the small things on earth,
The books, the papers, the old garters and union-suit buttons
Kept in a white cardboard box somewhere, and all the lower
Versions of cities flattened under the equalizing night.
The summer demands and takes away too much,
But night, the reserved, the reticent, gives more than it takes.

Worsening Situation

Like a rainstorm, he said, the braided colors
Wash over me and are no help. Or like one
At a feast who eats not, for he cannot choose
From among the smoking dishes. This severed hand
Stands for life, and wander as it will,
East or west, north or south, it is ever
A stranger who walks beside me. O seasons,
Booths, chaleur, dark-hatted charlatans
On the outskirts of some rural fete,
The name you drop and never say is mine, mine!
Some day I'll claim to you how all used up
I am because of you but in the meantime the ride
Continues. Everyone is along for the ride,
It seems. Besides, what else is there?
The annual games? True, there are occasions
For white uniforms and a special language
Kept secret from the others. The limes
Are duly sliced. I know all this
But can't seem to keep it from affecting me,
Every day, all day. I've tried recreation,
Reading until late at night, train rides
And romance.
                    One day a man called while I was out
And left this message: "You got the whole thing wrong
From start to finish. Luckily, there's still time
To correct the situation, but you must act fast.
See me at your earliest convenience. And please
Tell no one of this. Much besides your life depends on it."
I thought nothing of it at the time. Lately
I've been looking at old-fashioned plaids, fingering

Starched white collars, wondering whether there's a way
To get them really white again. My wife
Thinks I'm in Oslo—Oslo, France, that is.

Forties Flick

The shadow of the Venetian blind on the painted wall,
Shadows of the snake-plant and cacti, the plaster animals,
Focus the tragic melancholy of the bright stare
Into nowhere, a hole like the black holes in space.
In bra and panties she sidles to the window:
Zip! Up with the blind. A fragile street scene offers itself,
With wafer-thin pedestrians who know where they are going.
The blind comes down slowly, the slats are slowly tilted up.

Why must it always end this way?
A dais with woman reading, with the ruckus of her hair
And all that is unsaid about her pulling us back to her, with her
Into the silence that night alone can't explain.
Silence of the library, of the telephone with its pad,
But we didn't have to reinvent these either:
They had gone away into the plot of a story,
The "art" part—knowing what important details to leave out
And the way character is developed. Things too real
To be of much concern, hence artificial, yet now all over the page,
The indoors with the outside becoming part of you
As you find you had never left off laughing at death,
The background, dark vine at the edge of the porch.

As You Came from the Holy Land

of western New York state
were the graves all right in their bushings
was there a note of panic in the late August air
because the old man had peed in his pants again
was there turning away from the late afternoon glare
as though it too could be wished away
was any of this present
and how could this be
the magic solution to what you are in now
whatever has held you motionless
like this so long through the dark season
until now the women come out in navy blue
and the worms come out of the compost to die
it is the end of any season

you reading there so accurately
sitting not wanting to be disturbed
as you came from that holy land
what other signs of earth's dependency were upon you
what fixed sign at the crossroads
what lethargy in the avenues
where all is said in a whisper
what tone of voice among the hedges
what tone under the apple trees
the numbered land stretches away
and your house is built in tomorrow
but surely not before the examination
of what is right and will befall
not before the census
and the writing down of names

remember you are free to wander away
as from other times other scenes that were taking place
the history of someone who came too late
the time is ripe now and the adage
is hatching as the seasons change and tremble
it is finally as though that thing of monstrous interest
were happening in the sky
but the sun is setting and prevents you from seeing it

out of night the token emerges
its leaves like birds alighting all at once under a tree
taken up and shaken again
put down in weak rage
knowing as the brain does it can never come about
not here not yesterday in the past
only in the gap of today filling itself
as emptiness is distributed
in the idea of what time it is
when that time is already past

A Man of Words

His case inspires interest
But little sympathy; it is smaller
Than at first appeared. Does the first nettle
Make any difference as what grows
Becomes a skit? Three sides enclosed,
The fourth open to a wash of the weather,
Exits and entrances, gestures theatrically meant
To punctuate like doubled-over weeds as
The garden fills up with snow?
Ah, but this would have been another, quite other
Entertainment, not the metallic taste
In my mouth as I look away, density black as gunpowder
In the angles where the grass writing goes on,
Rose-red in unexpected places like the pressure
Of fingers on a book suddenly snapped shut.

Those tangled versions of the truth are
Combed out, the snarls ripped out
And spread around. Behind the mask
Is still a continental appreciation
Of what is fine, rarely appears and when it does is already
Dying on the breeze that brought it to the threshold
Of speech. The story worn out from telling.
All diaries are alike, clear and cold, with
The outlook for continued cold. They are placed
Horizontal, parallel to the earth,
Like the unencumbering dead. Just time to reread this
And the past slips through your fingers, wishing you were there.

Scheherazade

Unsupported by reason's enigma
Water collects in squared stone catch basins.
The land is dry. Under it moves
The water. Fish live in the wells. The leaves,
A concerned green, are scrawled on the light. Bad
Bindweed and rank ragweed somehow forget to flourish here.
An inexhaustible wardrobe has been placed at the disposal
Of each new occurrence. It can be itself now.
Day is almost reluctant to decline
And slowing down opens out new avenues
That don't infringe on space but are living here with us.
Other dreams came and left while the bank
Of colored verbs and adjectives was shrinking from the light
To nurse in shade their want of a method
But most of all she loved the particles
That transform objects of the same category
Into particular ones, each distinct
Within and apart from its own class.
In all this springing up was no hint
Of a tide, only a pleasant wavering of the air
In which all things seemed present, whether
Just past or soon to come. It was all invitation.
So much the flowers outlined along the night
Alleys when few were visible, yet
Their story sounded louder than the hum
Of bug and stick noises that brought up the rear,
Trundling it along into a new fact of day.
These were meant to be read as any
Salutation before getting down to business,
But they stuck to their guns, and so much
Was their obstinacy in keeping with the rest
(Like long flashes of white birds that refuse to die

When day does) that none knew the warp
Which presented this major movement as a firm
Digression, a plain that slowly becomes a mountain.

So each found himself caught in a net
As a fashion, and all efforts to wriggle free
Involved him further, inexorably, since all
Existed there to be told, shot through
From border to border. Here were stones
That read as patches of sunlight, there was the story
Of the grandparents, of the vigorous young champion
(The lines once given to another, now
Restored to the new speaker), dinners and assemblies,
The light in the old home, the secret way
The rooms fed into each other, but all
Was wariness of time watching itself
For nothing in the complex story grew outside:
The greatness in the moment of telling stayed unresolved
Until its wealth of incident, pain mixed with pleasure,
Faded in the precise moment of bursting
Into bloom, its growth a static lament.

Some stories survived the dynasty of the builders
But their echo was itself locked in, became
Anticipation that was only memory after all,
For the possibilities are limited. It is seen
At the end that the kind and good are rewarded,
That the unjust one is doomed to burn forever
Around his error, sadder and wiser anyway.
Between these extremes the others muddle through
Like us, uncertain but wearing artlessly
Their function of minor characters who must
Be kept in mind. It is we who make this
Jungle and call it space, naming each root,
Each serpent, for the sound of the name

As it clinks dully against our pleasure,
Indifference that is pleasure. And what would they be
Without an audience to restrict the innumerable
Passes and swipes, restored to good humor as it issues
Into the impervious evening air? So in some way
Although the arithmetic is incorrect
The balance is restored because it
Balances, knowing it prevails,
And the man who made the same mistake twice is exonerated.

Absolute Clearance

"Voilà, Messieurs, les spectacles que Dieu donne à l'univers…"
—*Bossuet*

He sees the pictures on the walls.
A sample of the truth only.
But one never has enough.
The truth doesn't satisfy.

In some vague hotel room
The linear blotches when dusk
Lifted them up were days and nights

And out over the ocean
The wish persisted to be a dream at home
Cloud or bird asleep in the trough
Of discursive waters.

The times when a slow horse along
A canal bank seems irrelevant and the truth:
The best in its best sample
Of time in relation to other time.

Suffer again the light to be displaced
To go down fuming
"So much is his courage high,
So vast his intelligence,
So glorious his destinies.

"Like an eagle that one sees always
Whether flying in the middle airs
Or alighting on some rock
Give piercing looks on all sides

To fall so surely on its prey
That one can avoid its nails
No less than its eyes."

How it would be clearer
Just to loaf, imagining little
(The fur of a cat in the sun):
Let the column of figures
Shift, add and subtract itself
(Sticks, numbers, letters)
And so on to median depth...

Until a room in some town
The result of a meeting therein
Clasping, unclasping
Toward the flustered look
Of toys one day put away for the last time.

"I put away childish things.
It was for this I came to Riverside
And lived here for three years
Now coming to a not uncertain
Ending or flowering as some would call it."

Teasing the blowing light
With its ultimate assurance
Severity of its curved smile
"Like the eagle
That hangs and hangs, then drops."

Grand Galop

All things seem mention of themselves
And the names which stem from them branch out to other referents.
Hugely, spring exists again. The weigela does its dusty thing
In fire-hammered air. And garbage cans are heaved against
The railing as the tulips yawn and crack open and fall apart.
And today is Monday. Today's lunch is: Spanish omelet, lettuce and
    tomato salad,
Jello, milk and cookies. Tomorrow's: sloppy joe on bun,
Scalloped corn, stewed tomatoes, rice pudding and milk.
The names we stole don't remove us:
We have moved on a little ahead of them
And now it is time to wait again.
Only waiting, the waiting: what fills up the time between?
It is another kind of wait, waiting for the wait to be ended.
Nothing takes up its fair share of time,
The wait is built into the things just coming into their own.
Nothing is partially incomplete, but the wait
Invests everything like a climate.
What time of day is it?
Does anything matter?
Yes, for you must wait to see what it is really like,
This event rounding the corner
Which will be unlike anything else and really
Cause no surprise: it's too ample.

Water
Drops from an air conditioner
On those who pass underneath. It's one of the sights of our town.
Puaagh. Vomit. Puaaaaagh. More vomit. One who comes
Walking dog on leash is distant to say how all this
Changes the minute to an hour, the hour
To the times of day, days to months, those easy-to-grasp entities,

And the months to seasons, which are far other, foreign
To our concept of time. Better the months—
They are almost persons—than these abstractions
That sift like marble dust across the unfinished works of the studio
Aging everything into a characterization of itself.
Better the cleanup committee concern itself with
Some item that is now little more than a feature
Of some obsolete style—cornice or spandrel
Out of the dimly remembered whole
Which probably lacks true distinction. But if one may pick it up,
Carry it over there, set it down,
Then the work is redeemed at the end
Under the smiling expanse of the sky
That plays no favorites but in the same way
Is honor only to those who have sought it.

The dog barks, the caravan passes on.
The words had a sort of bloom on them
But were weightless, carrying past what was being said.
"A nice time," you think, "to go out:
The early night is cool, but not
Too anything. People parading with their pets
Past lawns and vacant lots, as though these too were somehow
     imponderables
Before going home to the decency of one's private life
Shut up behind doors, which is nobody's business.
It does matter a little to the others
But only because it makes them realize how far their respect
Has brought them. No one would dare to intrude.
It is a night like many another
With the sky now a bit impatient for today to be over
Like a bored salesgirl shifting from foot to stockinged foot."
These khaki undershorts hung out on lines,
The wind billowing among them, are we never to make a statement?
And certain buildings we always pass which are never mentioned—

It's getting out of hand.
As long as one has some sense that each thing knows its place
All is well, but with the arrival and departure
Of each new one overlapping so intensely in the semi-darkness
It's a bit mad. Too bad, I mean, that getting to know each just for a
    fleeting second
Must be replaced by imperfect knowledge of the featureless whole,
Like some pocket history of the world, so general
As to constitute a sob or wail unrelated
To any attempt at definition. And the minor eras
Take on an importance out of all proportion to the story
For it can no longer unwind, but must be kept on hand
Indefinitely, like a first-aid kit no one ever uses
Or a word in the dictionary that no one will ever look up.
The custard is setting; meanwhile
I not only have my own history to worry about
But am forced to fret over insufficient details related to large
Unfinished concepts that can never bring themselves to the point
Of being, with or without my help, if any were forthcoming.

It is just the movement of the caravan away
Into an abstract night, with no
Precise goal in view, and indeed not caring,
That distributes this pause. Why be in a hurry
To speed away in the opposite direction, toward the other end of
    infinity?
For things can harden meaningfully in the moment of indecision.
I cannot decide in which direction to walk
But this doesn't matter to me, and I might as well
Decide to climb a mountain (it looks almost flat)
As decide to go home
Or to a bar or restaurant or to the home
Of some friend as charming and ineffectual as I am
Because these pauses are supposed to be life
And they sink steel needles deep into the pores, as though to say

There is no use trying to escape
And it is all here anyway. And their steep, slippery sides defy
Any notion of continuity. It is this
That takes us back into what really is, it seems, history—
The lackluster, disorganized kind without dates
That speaks out of the hollow trunk of a tree
To warn away the merely polite, or those whose destiny
Leaves them no time to quibble about the means,
Which are not ends, and yet... What precisely is it
About the time of day it is, the weather, that causes people to note it
 painstakingly in their diaries
For them to read who shall come after?
Surely it is because the ray of light
Or gloom striking you this moment is hope
In all its mature, matronly form, taking all things into account
And reapportioning them according to size
So that if one can't say that this is the natural way
It should have happened, at least one can have no cause for
 complaint
Which is the same as having reached the end, wise
In that expectation and enhanced by its fulfillment, or the absence
 of it.
But we say, it cannot come to any such end
As long as we are left around with no place to go.
And yet it has ended, and the thing we have fulfilled we have
 become.

Now it is the impulse of morning that makes
My watch tick. As one who pokes his head
Out from under a pile of blankets, the good and bad together,
So this tangle of impossible resolutions and irresolutions:
The desire to have fun, to make noise, and so to
Add to the already all-but-illegible scrub forest of graffiti on the
 shithouse wall.
Someone is coming to get you:

The mailman, or a butler enters with a letter on a tray
Whose message is to change everything, but in the meantime
One is to worry about one's smell or dandruff or lost glasses—
If only the curtain-raiser would end, but it is interminable.
But there is this consolation:
If it turns out to be not worth doing, I haven't done it;
If the sight appalls me, I have seen nothing;
If the victory is pyrrhic, I haven't won it.
And so from a day replete with rumors
Of things being done on the other side of the mountains
A nucleus remains, a still-perfect possibility
That can be kept indefinitely. And yet
The groans of labor pains are deafening; one must
Get up, get out and be on with it. Morning is for sissies like you
But the real trials, the ones that separate the men from the boys,
        come later.

Oregon was kinder to us. The streets
Offered a variety of directions to the foot
And bookstores where pornography is sold. But then
One whiffs just a slight odor of madness in the air.
They all got into their cars and drove away
As in the end of a movie. So that it finally made no difference
Whether this were the end or it was somewhere else:
If it had to be somewhere it might as well be
Here, on top of one. Here, as elsewhere,
April advances new suggestions, and one may as well
Move along with them, especially in view of
The midnight-blue light that in turning itself inside out
Offers something strange to the attention, a thing
That is not itself, gnat whirling before my eyes
At an incredible, tame velocity. Too pronounced after all
To be that meaningless. And so on to afternoon
On the desert, with oneself cleaned up, and the location
Almost brand-new what with the removal of gum wrappers, etc.

But I was trying to tell you about a strange thing
That happened to me, but this is no way to tell about it,
By making it truly happen. It drifts away in fragments.
And one is left sitting in the yard
To try to write poetry
Using what Wyatt and Surrey left around,
Took up and put down again
Like so much gorgeous raw material,
As though it would always happen in some way
And meanwhile since we are all advancing
It is sure to come about in spite of everything
On a Sunday, where you are left sitting
In the shade that, as always, is just a little too cool.
So there is whirling out at you from the not deep
Emptiness the word "cock" or some other, brother and sister words
With not much to be expected from them, though these
Are the ones that waited so long for you and finally left, having
      given up hope.
There is a note of desperation in one's voice, pleading for them,
And meanwhile the intensity thins and sharpens
Its point, that is the thing it was going to ask.
One has been waiting around all evening for it
Before sleep had stopped definitively the eyes and ears
Of all those who came as an audience.
Still, that poetry does sometimes occur
If only in creases in forgotten letters
Packed away in trunks in the attic—things you forgot you had
And what would it matter anyway,
That recompense so precisely dosed
As to seem the falling true of a perverse judgment.
You forget how there could be a gasp of a new air
Hidden in that jumble. And of course your forgetting
Is a sign of just how much it matters to you:
"It must have been important."
The lies fall like flaxen threads from the skies

All over America, and the fact that some of them are true of course
Doesn't so much not matter as serve to justify
The whole mad organizing force under the billows of correct
    delight.
Surrey, your lute is getting an attack of nervous paralysis
But there are, again, things to be sung of
And this is one of them, only I would not dream of intruding on
The frantic completeness, the all-purpose benevolence
Of that still-moist garden where the tooting originates:
Between intervals of clenched teeth, your venomous rondelay.

Ask a hog what is happening. Go on. Ask him.
The road just seems to vanish
And not that far in the distance, either. The horizon must have been
    moved up.
So it is that by limping carefully
From one day to the next, one approaches a worn, round stone
    tower
Crouching low in the hollow of a gully
With no door or window but a lot of old license plates
Tacked up over a slit too narrow for a wrist to pass through
And a sign: "Van Camp's Pork and Beans."
From then on in: *angst*-colored skies, emotional withdrawals
As the whole business starts to frighten even you,
Its originator and promoter. The horizon returns
As a smile of recognition this time, polite, unquestioning.
How long ago high school graduation seems
Yet it cannot have been so very long:
One has traveled such a short distance.
The styles haven't changed much,
And I still have a sweater and one or two other things I had then.
It seems only yesterday that we saw
The movie with the cows in it
And turned to one at your side, who burped
As morning saw a new garnet-and-pea-green order propose

Itself out of the endless bathos, like science-fiction lumps.
Impossible not to be moved by the tiny number
Those people wore, indicating they should be raised to this or that
     power.
But now we are at Cape Fear and the overland trail
Is impassable, and a dense curtain of mist hangs over the sea.

Poem in Three Parts

1. Love

"Once I let a guy blow me.
I kind of backed away from the experience.
Now years later, I think of it
Without emotion. There has been no desire to repeat,
No hangups either. Probably if the circumstances were right
It could happen again, but I don't know,
I just have other things to think about,
More important things. Who goes to bed with what
Is unimportant. Feelings are important.
Mostly I think of feelings, they fill up my life
Like the wind, like tumbling clouds
In a sky full of clouds, clouds upon clouds."

Nameless shrubs running across a field
That didn't drain last year and
Isn't draining this year to fall short
Like waves at the end of a lake,
Each with a little sigh,
Are you sure this is what the pure day
With its standing light intends?
There are so many different jobs:
It's sufficient to choose one, or a fraction of one.
Days will be blue elsewhere with their own purpose.
One must bear in mind one thing.
It isn't necessary to know what that thing is.
All things are palpable, none are known.
The day fries, with a fine conscience,
Shadows, ripples, underbrush, old cars.

The conscience is to you as what is known,
The unknowable gets to be known.
Familiar things seem a long way off.

2. Courage

In a diamond-paned checked shirt
To be setting out this way:
A blah morning
Not too far from home (home
Is a modest one-bedroom apartment,
City-owned and operated),
The average debris of the journey
Less than at first thought,
Smell of open water,
Troughs, special pits.
It all winds back again
In time for evening's torque:
So much we could have done,
So much we did do.
Weeds like skyscrapers against the blue vault of heaven:
Where is it to end? What is this? Who are these people?
Am I myself, or a talking tree?

3. I Love the Sea

There is no promise but lots
Of intimacy the way yellowed land narrows together.
This part isn't very popular
For some reason: the houses need repairs,
The cars in the yards are too new.
The enclosing slopes dream and are forgetful.
There are joyous, warm patches
Amid nondescript trees.

My dream gets obtuse:
When I woke up this morning I noticed first
That you weren't there, then prodded
Slowly back into the dream:
These trains, people, beaches, rides
In happiness because their variety
Is outlived but still there, outside somewhere,
In the side yard, maybe.

Ivy is blanketing one whole wall.
The time is darker
For fast reasons into everything, about what concerns it now.
We could sleep together again but that wouldn't
Bring back the profit of these dangerous dreams of the sea,
All that crashing, that blindness, that blood
One associates with other days near the sea
Although it persists, like the blindness of noon.

Voyage in the Blue

As on a festal day in early spring
The tidelands maneuver and the air is quick with imitations:
Ships, hats appear. And those,
The mind-readers, who are never far off. But
To get to know them we must avoid them.

And so, into our darkness life seeps,
Keeping its part of the bargain. But what of
Houses, standing ruined, desolate just now:
Is this not also beautiful and wonderful?
For where a mirage has once been, life must be.

The pageant, growing ever more curious, reaches
An ultimate turning point. Now everything is going to be
Not dark, but on the contrary, charged with so much light
It looks dark, because things are now packed so closely
        together.
We see it with our teeth. And once this

Distant corner is rounded, everything
Is not to be made new again. We shall be inhabited
In the old way, as ideal things came to us,
Yet in the having we shall be growing, rising above it
Into an admixture of deep blue enameled sky and bristly
        gold stars.

The way the date came in
Made no sense, it never had any.
It should have been a caution to you
To listen more carefully to the words
Under the wind as it moved toward us.

Perhaps, sinking into the pearl stain of that passionate eye
The minutes came to seem the excrement of all they were passing
    through,
A time when colors no longer mattered.
They are to us as qualities we were not meant to catch
As being too far removed from our closed-in state.

And ideally the chime of this
Will come to have the fascination of a remembered thing
Without avatars, or so remote, like a catastrophe
In some unheard-of country, that our concern
Will be only another fact in a long list of important facts.

You and I and the dog
Are here, this is what matters for now.
In other times things will happen that cannot possibly involve
    us now
And this is good, a true thing, perpendicular to the ground
Like the freshest, least complicated and earliest of memories.

We have them all, those people, and now they have us.
Their decision was limited, waiting for us to make the first move.
But now that we have done so the results are unfathomable, as
    though
A single implication could sway the whole universe on its stem.
We are fashionably troubled by this new edge of what had seemed
    finite

Before and now seems infinite though encircled by gradual doubts
Of whatever came over us. Perhaps the old chic was less barren,
More something to be looked forward to, than this
Morning in the orchards under an unclouded sky,
This painful freshness of each thing being exactly itself.

Perhaps all that is wanted is time.
People cover us, they are older
And have lived before. They want no part of us,
Only to be dying, and over with it.
Out of step with all that is passing along with them

But living with it deep into the midst of things.
It is civilization that counts, after all, they seem
To be saying, and we are as much a part of it as anybody else
Only we think less about it, even not at all, until some
Fool comes shouting into the forest at nightfall

News of some thing we know and care little of,
As the distant castle rejoices to the joyous
Sound of hooves, releasing rooks straight up into the faultless air
And meanwhile weighs its shadow ever heavier on the mirroring
Surface of the river, surrounding the little boat with three figures
    in it.

Farm

A protracted wait that is also night.
Funny how the white fence posts
Go on and on, a quiet reproach
That goes under as day ends
Though the geometry remains,
A thing like nudity at the end
Of a long stretch. "It makes such a difference."
OK. So is the "really not the same thing at all,"
Viewed through the wrong end of a telescope
And holding up that bar.

Living with the girl
Got kicked into the sod of things.
There was a to-do end of June,
Comings and goings
Before the matter is dropped.
But it stays around, like her faint point
Of frown, or the dripping leaves
Of pie-plant and hollyhock,
Also momentary in defeat.
No one has the last laugh.

Farm II

I was thinking
Now that the flowers are
                              forgotten
A whole new frontier
Backing around the old one are
Swamping its former good ideas
Plowing under the errors too
In its tin maelstrom: the overloaded
Ferryboat slowly moves away from the dock
Are these dog-eared things

Weeds what you call them
These things sitting like mail to be read
Toward the end of afternoon
Things the mailman brought

I would like to enroll
In the new course
At the study center

A lattice-work crust
Holes are blobs of darkness
Has been placed across the road
You can't walk out too far that way any more
They say the children are demolishing
The insides of the woods
                              burnt orange
That it's spectacular

But it doesn't
Take us out into the open sea
Only to the middle of a river
Fumbling which way to go.

Farm III

Small waves strike
The dark stones. The wife reads
The letter. There is nothing irreversible:
Points to the last sibilants
Of invading beef and calico.

Pretty soon oil has
Taken up the place of
The dark around you. It was all
As told, but anyway it never came out just right:
A fraction here, a lisp where it didn't matter.
It has to be presented
Through a final gap: pear trees and flowers
An ultimate resinous wall
Basking in the temperate climate
Of your identity. Sullen fecundity
To be watched over.

Hop o' My Thumb

The grand hotels, dancing girls
Urge forward under a veil of "lost illusion"
The deed to this day or some other day.
There is no day in the calendar
The dairy company sent out
That lets you possess it wildly like
The body of a dreaming woman in a dream:
All flop over at the top when seized,
The stem too slender, the top too loose and heavy,
Blushing with fine foliage of dreams.
The motor cars, tinsel hats,
Supper of cakes, the amorous children
Take the solitary downward path of dreams
And are not seen again.
What is it, Undine?
The notes now can scarcely be heard
In the hubbub of the flattening storm,
With the third wish unspoken.

I remember meeting you in a dark dream
Of April, you or some girl,
The necklace of wishes alive and breathing around your throat.
In the blindness of that dark whose
Brightness turned to sand salt-glazed in noon sun
We could not know each other or know which part
Belonged to the other, pelted in an electric storm of rain.
Only gradually the mounds that meant our bodies
That wore our selves concaved into view
But intermittently as through dark mist
Smeared against fog. No worse time to have come,
Yet all was desiring though already desired and past,

The moment a monument to itself
No one would ever see or know was there.

That time faded too and the night
Softened to smooth spirals or foliage at night.
There were sleeping cabins near by, blind lanterns,
Nocturnal friendliness of the plate of milk left for the fairies
Who otherwise might be less well disposed:
Friendship of white sheets patched with milk.
And always an open darkness in which one name
Cries over and over again: Ariane! Ariane!
Was it for this you led your sisters back from sleep
And now he of the blue beard has outmaneuvered you?
But for the best perhaps: let
Those sisters slink into the sapphire
Hair that is mounting day.
There are still other made-up countries
Where we can hide forever,
Wasted with eternal desire and sadness,
Sucking the sherbets, crooning the tunes, naming the names.

De Imagine Mundi

The many as noticed by the one:
The noticed one, confusing itself with the many
Yet perceives itself as an individual
Traveling between two fixed points.
Such glance as dares dart out
To pin you in your afternoon lair is only a reflex,
A speech in a play consisting entirely of stage directions
Because there happened to be a hole for it there.
Unfortunately, fewer than one half of one per cent
Recognized the divined gesture as currency
(Which it is, albeit inflated)
And the glance comes to rest on top of a steeple
With about as much interest as a bird's.

They had moved out here from Boston
Those two. (The one, a fair sample
Of the fair-sheaved many,
The other boggling into single oddness
Plays at it when he must
Not getting better or younger.)

The weather kept them at their small tasks:
Sorting out the news, mending this and that.
The great poker face impinged on them. And rejoiced
To be a living reproach to
Something new they've got.
Skeeter collecting info: "Did you know
About the Mugwump of the Final Hour?"
Their even flesh tone
A sign of "Day off,"
The buses moving along quite quickly on the nearby island
Also registered, as per his plan.

Taking a path you never saw before
Thought you knew the area
(The many perceive they fight off sleep).
"A few gaffers stay on
To the end of the line
Tho that is between bookends."
The note is struck finally
With just sufficient force but like a thunderbolt
As only the loudest can be imagined.
And they stay on to talk it over.

Foreboding

A breeze off the lake—petal-shaped
Luna-park effects avoid the teasing outline
Of where we would be if we were here.
Bombed out of our minds, I think
The way here is too close, too packed
With surges of feeling. It can't be.
The wipeout occurs first at the center,
Now around the edges. A big ugly one
With braces kicking the shit out of a smaller one
Who reaches for a platinum axe stamped excalibur:
Just jungles really. The daytime bars are
Packed but night has more meaning
In the pockets and side vents. I feel as though
Somebody had just brought me an equation.
I say, "I can't answer this—I know
That it's true, please believe me,
I can see the proof, lofty, invisible
In the sky far above the striped awnings. I just see
That I want it to go on, without
Anybody's getting hurt, and for the shuffling
To resume between me and my side of night."

The Tomb of Stuart Merrill

It is the first soir of March
They have taken the plants away.

Martha Hoople wanted a big "gnossienne" hydrangea
Smelling all over of Jicky for her
Card party: the basement couldn't
Hold up all that wildness.

The petits fours have left.

Then up and spake the Major:
The new conservatism is
Sitting down beside you.
Once when the bus slid out past Place Pereire
I caught the lens-cover reflection: lilacs
Won't make much difference it said.

Otherwise in Paris why
You never approved much of my pet remedies.
I spoke once of a palliative for piles
You wouldn't try or admit to trying any other.
Now we live without or rather we get along without
Each other. Each of us does
Live within that conundrum
We don't call living
Both shut up and open.
Can knowledge ever be harmful?
How about a mandate? I think
Of throwing myself on the mercy of the court.

They are bringing the plants back
One by one
In the interstices of heaven, earth and today.

"I have become attracted to your style. You seem to possess within
your work an air of total freedom of expression and imagery, some-
what interesting and puzzling. After I read one of your poems, I'm
always tempted to read and reread it. It seems that my inexperience
holds me back from understanding your meanings.

"I really would like to know what it is you do to 'magnetize' your
poetry, where the curious reader, always a bit puzzled, comes back
for a clearer insight."

The canons are falling
One by one
Including *"le célèbre"* of Pachelbel
The final movement of Franck's sonata for piano and violin.
How about a new kind of hermetic conservatism
And suffering withdrawal symptoms of same?

Let's get on with it
But what about the past

Because it only builds up out of fragments.
Each evening we walk out to see
How they are coming along with the temple.
There is an interest in watching how
One piece is added to another.
At least it isn't horrible like
Being inside a hospital and really finding out
What it's like in there.

So one is tempted not to include this page
In the fragment of our lives
Just as its meaning is about to coagulate
In the air around us:

"Father!" "Son!" "Father I thought we'd lost you
In the blue and buff planes of the Aegean:
Now it seems you're really back."
"Only for a while, son, only for a while."
We can go inside now.

Tarpaulin

Easing the thing
Into spurts of activity
Before the emptiness of late afternoon
Is a kind of will power
Blaring back its received vision
From a thousand tenement windows
Just before night
Its signal fading

River

It thinks itself too good for
These generalizations and is
Moved on by them. The opposite side
Is plunged in shade, this one
In self-esteem. But the center
Keeps collapsing and re-forming.
The couple at a picnic table (but
It's too early in the season for picnics)
Are traipsed across by the river's
Unknowing knowledge of its workings
To avoid possible boredom and the stain
Of too much intuition the whole scene
Is walled behind glass. "Too early,"
She says, "in the season." A hawk drifts by.
"Send everybody back to the city."

Mixed Feelings

A pleasant smell of frying sausages
Attacks the sense, along with an old, mostly invisible
Photograph of what seems to be girls lounging around
An old fighter bomber, circa 1942 vintage.
How to explain to these girls, if indeed that's what they are,
These Ruths, Lindas, Pats and Sheilas
About the vast change that's taken place
In the fabric of our society, altering the texture
Of all things in it? And yet
They somehow look as if they knew, except
That it's so hard to see them, it's hard to figure out
Exactly what kind of expressions they're wearing.
What are your hobbies, girls? Aw nerts,
One of them might say, this guy's too much for me.
Let's go on and out, somewhere
Through the canyons of the garment center
To a small café and have a cup of coffee.
I am not offended that these creatures (that's the word)
Of my imagination seem to hold me in such light esteem,
Pay so little heed to me. It's part of a complicated
Flirtation routine, anyhow, no doubt. But this talk of
The garment center? Surely that's California sunlight
Belaboring them and the old crate on which they
Have draped themselves, fading its Donald Duck insignia
To the extreme point of legibility.
Maybe they were lying but more likely their
Tiny intelligences cannot retain much information.
Not even one fact, perhaps. That's why
They think they're in New York. I like the way
They look and act and feel. I wonder
How they got that way, but am not going to
Waste any more time thinking about them.

I have already forgotten them
Until some day in the not too distant future
When we meet possibly in the lounge of a modern airport,
They looking as astonishingly young and fresh as when this picture
    was made
But full of contradictory ideas, stupid ones as well as
Worthwhile ones, but all flooding the surface of our minds
As we babble about the sky and the weather and the forests of
    change.

The One Thing That Can Save America

Is anything central?
Orchards flung out on the land,
Urban forests, rustic plantations, knee-high hills?
Are place names central?
Elm Grove, Adcock Corner, Story Book Farm?
As they concur with a rush at eye level
Beating themselves into eyes which have had enough
Thank you, no more thank you.
And they come on like scenery mingled with darkness
The damp plains, overgrown suburbs,
Places of known civic pride, of civil obscurity.

These are connected to my version of America
But the juice is elsewhere.
This morning as I walked out of your room
After breakfast crosshatched with
Backward and forward glances, backward into light,
Forward into unfamiliar light,
Was it our doing, and was it
The material, the lumber of life, or of lives
We were measuring, counting?
A mood soon to be forgotten
In crossed girders of light, cool downtown shadow
In this morning that has seized us again?

I know that I braid too much my own
Snapped-off perceptions of things as they come to me.
They are private and always will be.
Where then are the private turns of event
Destined to boom later like golden chimes
Released over a city from a highest tower?
The quirky things that happen to me, and I tell you,

And you instantly know what I mean?
What remote orchard reached by winding roads
Hides them? Where are these roots?

It is the lumps and trials
That tell us whether we shall be known
And whether our fate can be exemplary, like a star.
All the rest is waiting
For a letter that never arrives,
Day after day, the exasperation
Until finally you have ripped it open not knowing what it is,
The two envelope halves lying on a plate.
The message was wise, and seemingly
Dictated a long time ago.
Its truth is timeless, but its time has still
Not arrived, telling of danger, and the mostly limited
Steps that can be taken against danger
Now and in the future, in cool yards,
In quiet small houses in the country,
Our country, in fenced areas, in cool shady streets.

Tenth Symphony

I have not told you
About the riffraff at the boat show.
But seeing the boats coast by
Just now on their truck:
All red and white and blue and red
Prompts me to, wanting to get in your way.

You've never told me about a lot of things:
Why you love me, why we love you, and just exactly
What sex is. When people speak of it
As happens increasingly, are they always
Referring to the kind where sexual organs are brought in—
Diffident, vague, hard to imagine as they are to a blind person?
I find that thinking these things divides us,
Brings us together. As on last Thanksgiving
Nobody could finish what was on his plate,
And gave thanks. Means more
To some than me I guess.
But again I'm not sure of that.

There is some connexion
(I like the way the English spell it
They're so clever about some things
Probably smarter generally than we are
Although there is supposed to be something
We have that they don't—don't ask me
What it is. And please no talk of openness.
I would pick Francis Thompson over Bret Harte
Any day, if I had to)
Among this. It connects up,
Not *to* anything, but kind of like
Closing the ranks so as to leave them open.

You can "stop and shop." Self service
And the honor system prevail, resulting in
Tremendous amounts of spare time,
A boon to some, to others more of a problem
That only points a way around it.
Sitting in the living room this afternoon I saw
How to use it. My vision remained etched in the
Buff wall a long time, an elective
Cheshire cat. Unable to cancel,
The message is received penultimately.

So over these past years—
A little puttering around,
Some relaxing, a lot of plans and ideas.
Hope to have more time to tell you about
The latter in the foreseeable future.

On Autumn Lake

Leading liot act to foriage is activity
Of Chinese philosopher here on Autumn Lake thoughtfully
    inserted in
Plovince of Quebec—stop it! I will not. The edge hugs
The lake with ever-more-paternalistic insistence, whose effect
Is in the blue way up ahead. The distance

By air from other places to here isn't much, but
It doesn't count, at least not the way the
Shore distance—leaf, tree, stone; optional (fern, frog, skunk);
And then stone, tree, leaf; then another optional—counts.
It's like the "machines" of the 19th-century Academy.
Turns out you didn't need all that training
To do art—that it was even better not to have it. Look at
The Impressionists—some of 'em had it, too, but preferred to
    forget it
In vast composed canvases by turns riotous
And indigent in color, from which only the notion of space is lacking.

I do not think that this
Will be my last trip to Autumn Lake
Have some friends among many severe heads
We all scholars sitting under tree
Waiting for nut to fall. Some of us studying
Persian and Aramaic, others the art of distilling
Weird fragrances out of nothing, from the ground up.
In each the potential is realized, the two wires
Are crossing.

Fear of Death

What is it now with me
And is it as I have become?
Is there no state free from the boundary lines
Of before and after? The window is open today

And the air pours in with piano notes
In its skirts, as though to say, "Look, John,
I've brought these and these"—that is,
A few Beethovens, some Brahmses,

A few choice Poulenc notes.... Yes,
It is being free again, the air, it has to keep coming back
Because that's all it's good for.
I want to stay with it out of fear

That keeps me from walking up certain steps,
Knocking at certain doors, fear of growing old
Alone, and of finding no one at the evening end
Of the path except another myself

Nodding a curt greeting: "Well, you've been awhile
But now we're back together, which is what counts."
Air in my path, you could shorten this,
But the breeze has dropped, and silence is the last word.

Ode to Bill

Some things we do take up a lot more time
And are considered a fruitful, natural thing to do.
I am coming out of one way to behave
Into a plowed cornfield. On my left, gulls,
On an inland vacation. They seem to mind the way
　　　I write.

Or, to take another example: last month
I vowed to write more. What is writing?
Well, in my case, it's getting down on paper
Not thoughts, exactly, but ideas, maybe:
Ideas about thoughts. Thoughts is too grand a word.
Ideas is better, though not precisely what I mean.
Someday I'll explain. Not today though.

I feel as though someone had made me a vest
Which I was wearing out of doors into the countryside
Out of loyalty to the person, although
There is no one to see, except me
With my inner vision of what I look like.
The wearing is both a duty and a pleasure
Because it absorbs me, absorbs me too much.

One horse stands out irregularly against
The land over there. And am I receiving
This vision? Is it mine, or do I already owe it
For other visions, unnoticed and unrecorded
On the great, relaxed curve of time,
All the forgotten springs, dropped pebbles,
Songs once heard that then passed out of light

Into everyday oblivion? He moves away slowly,
Looks up and pumps the sky, a lingering
Question. Him too we can sacrifice
To the end progress, for we must, we must be moving on.

Lithuanian Dance Band

Nathan the Wise is a good title it's a reintroduction
Of heavy seeds attached by toggle switch to long loops leading
Out of literature and life into worldly chaos in which
We struggle two souls out of work for it's a long way back to
The summation meanwhile we live in it "gradually getting used to"
Everything and this overrides living and is superimposed on it
As when a wounded jackal is tied to the waterhole the lion does come

I write you to air these few thoughts feelings you are
Most likely driving around the city in your little car
Breathing in the exquisite air of the city and the exhaust fumes dust
    and other
Which make it up only hold on awhile there will be time
For other decisions but now I want to concentrate on this
Image of you secure and projected how I imagine you
Because you are this way where are you you are in my thoughts

Something in me was damaged I don't know how or by what
Today is suddenly broad and a whole era of uncertainties is ending
Like World War I or the twenties it keeps ending this is the
    beginning
Of music afterward and refreshments all kinds of simple delicacies
That toast the heart and create a rival ambiance of cordiality
To the formal one we are keeping up in our hearts the same

What with skyscrapers and dirigibles and balloons the sky seems
    pretty crowded
And a nice place to live at least I think so do you
And the songs strike up there are chorales everywhere so pretty it's
    lovely
And everywhere the truth rushes in to fill the gaps left by

Its sudden demise so that a fairly accurate record of its activity is
    possible
If there were sex in friendship this would be the place to have it right
    here on this floor
With bells ringing and the loud music pealing

Perhaps another day one will want to review all this
For today it looks compressed like lines packed together
In one of those pictures you reflect with a polished tube
To get the full effect and this is possible
I feel it in the lean reaches of the weather and the wind
That sweeps articulately down these drab streets
Bringing everything to a high gloss

Yet we are alone too and that's sad isn't it
Yet you are meant to be alone at least part of the time
You must be in order to work and yet it always seems so unnatural
As though seeing people were intrinsic to life which it just might be
And then somehow the loneliness is more real and more human
You know not just the scarecrow but the whole landscape
And the crows peacefully pecking where the harrow has passed

Sand Pail

Process
of a red stripe through much whiplash
of environmental sweepstakes misinterprets
slabs as they come forward. A
footprint
directs traffic in the center
of flat crocus plaza as the storm
incurves on this new situation. Why
are there developments?
A transparent shovel paves, "they" say,
residual elastic fetters
pictures of moments
brought under the sand.

No Way of Knowing

And then? Colors and names of colors,
The knowledge of you a certain color had?
The whole song bag, the eternal oom-pah refrain?
Street scenes? A blur of pavement
After the cyclists passed, calling to each other,
Calling each other strange, funny-sounding names?
Yes, probably, but in the meantime, waking up
In the middle of a dream with one's mouth full
Of unknown words takes in all of these:
It is both the surface and the accidents
Scarring that surface, yet it too only contains
As a book on Sweden only contains the pages of that book.
The dank no-places and the insubstantial pinnacles—
Both get carried away on the surface of a flood
That doesn't care about anything,
Not even about minding its own business.
There were holidays past we used to
Match up, and yep, they fitted together
All right, but the days in between grow rank,
Consume their substance, orphan, disinherit
But the air stands in curtains, reigns
Like a centennial. No one can get in or out.
These are parts of the same body:
One could possibly live without some
Such as a finger or elbow, but the head is
Necessary, and what is in doubt here. This
Morning it was off taking French lessons.
Now it is resting and cannot be disturbed.

Yes, but—there are no "yes, buts"s.
The body is what this is all about and it disperses
In sheeted fragments, all somewhere around

But difficult to read correctly since there is
No common vantage point, no point of view
Like the "I" in a novel. And in truth
No one never saw the point of any. This stubble-field
Of witnessings and silent lowering of the lids
On angry screen-door moment rushing back
To the edge of woods was always alive with its own
Rigid binary system of inducing truths
From starved knowledge of them. It has worked
And will go on working. All attempts to influence
The working are parallelism, undulating, writhing
Sometimes but kept to the domain of metaphor.
There is no way of knowing whether these are
Our neighbors or friendly savages trapped in the distance
By the red tape of a mirage. The fact that
We drawled "hallo" to them just lazily enough this morning
Doesn't mean that a style was inaugurated. Anyway evening
Kind of changes things. Not the color,
The quality of a handshake, the edge on someone's breath,
So much as a general anxiety to get everything all added up,
Flowers arranged and out of sight. The vehicular madness
Goes on, crashing, thrashing away, but
For many this is near enough to the end: one may
Draw up a chair close to the balcony railing.
The sunset is just starting to light up.

As when the songs start to go
Not much can be done about it. Waiting
In vanilla corridors for an austere
Young nurse to appear, an opaque glass vase of snapdragons
On one arm, the dangerously slender heroine
Backbending over the other, won't save the denouement
Already drenched in the perfume of fatality. The passengers
Reappear. The cut driver pushes them to heaven.
(Waterford explodes over the flagstones.)

At the same time that we are trying to spell out
This very simple word, put one note
After the other, push back the dead chaos
Insinuating itself in the background like mists
Of happy autumn fields—your money is dead.
I like the spirit of the songs, though,
The camaraderie that is the last thing to peel off,
Visible even now on the woven pattern of branches
And twilight. Why must you go? Why can't you
Spend the night, here in my bed, with my arms wrapped tightly
    around you?
Surely that would solve everything by supplying
A theory of knowledge on a scale with the gigantic
Bits and pieces of knowledge we have retained:
An LP record of all your favorite friendships,
Of letters from the front? Too
Fantastic to make sense? But it made the chimes ring.
If you listen you can hear them ringing still:
A mood, a Stimmung, adding up to a sense of what they really were,
All along, through the chain of lengthening days.

Suite

The inert lifeless mass calls out into space:
Seven long years and the wall hasn't been built yet
The crust thickens, the back of everything...
Clustered carillons and the pink dew of afterthoughts
Support it.

This was to be forgotten, eliminated
From history. But time is a garden wherein
Memories thrive monstrously until
They become the vagrant flowering of something else
Like stopping near the fence with your raincoat.

At night, orange mists.
The sun has killed a trillion of 'em
And it keeps stretching back, impossible planets.
How do I know? I'm lost. It says its name.
The blue-black message at the end of the garden
Is garbled. Meanwhile we're supposed to be here
Among pine trees and nice breaths of fresh air.

Snow was the last thing he'd expected.
Sun, and the kiss of far, unfamiliar lands,
Harsh accents though strangely kind
And now from the unbuttoned corner moving out,
Coming out, the postponed play of this day.
Astonishing. It really tells you about yourself,
The day made whole, the eye and the report together, silent.

Märchenbilder

Es war einmal... No, it's too heavy
To be said. Besides, you aren't paying attention any more.
How shall I put it?
"The rain thundered on the uneven red flagstones.

The steadfast tin soldier gazed beyond the drops
Remembering the hat-shaped paper boat, that soon..."
That's not it either.
Think about the long summer evenings of the past, the queen
    anne's lace.

Sometimes a musical phrase would perfectly sum up
The mood of a moment. One of those lovelorn sonatas
For wind instruments was riding past on a solemn white horse.
Everybody wondered who the new arrival was.

Pomp of flowers, decorations
Junked next day. Now look out of the window.
The sky is clear and bland. The wrong kind of day
For business or games, or betting on a sure thing.

The trees weep drops
Into the water at night. Slowly couples gather.
She looks into his eyes. "It would not be good
To be left alone." He: "I'll stay

As long as the night allows." This was one of those night
    rainbows
In negative color. As we advance, it retreats; we see
We are now far into a cave, must be. Yet there seem to be
Trees all around, and a wind lifts their leaves, slightly.

I want to go back, out of the bad stories,
But there's always the possibility that the next one...
No, it's another almond tree, or a ring-swallowing frog...
Yet they are beautiful as we people them

With ourselves. They are empty as cupboards.
To spend whole days drenched in them, waiting for the next
    whisper,
For the word in the next room. This is how the princes must have
    behaved,
Lying down in the frugality of sleep.

City Afternoon

A veil of haze protects this
Long-ago afternoon forgotten by everybody
In this photograph, most of them now
Sucked screaming through old age and death.

If one could seize America
Or at least a fine forgetfulness
That seeps into our outline
Defining our volumes with a stain
That is fleeting too

But commemorates
Because it does define, after all:
Gray garlands, that threesome
Waiting for the light to change,
Air lifting the hair of one
Upside down in the reflecting pool.

Robin Hood's Barn

This would be the day: a few small drops of rain,
A dab of this, a touch of eau-de-cologne air
As long as it's suggestive. And it
Mounts, a serenade, to the surrounding
Love. You bad birds,
But God shall not punish you, you
Shall be with us in heaven, though less
Conscious of your happiness, perhaps, than we.
Hell is a not quite satisfactory heaven, probably,
But you are the fruit and jewels
Of my arrangement: O be with me!
Forget stand-offishness, exact
Bookkeeping of harsh terms! The banal
Sun is about to creep across heaven on its
Daily turn: don't let it find us arguing
Or worse, alone, each
Having turned his back to the other,
Alone in the wonderful solitude
Of the new day. To be there
Is not to know it, its outline
Creeps up on you, and then it has fallen over you
Like bedclothes of fog.
From some serene, high table
Set near the top of a flight of stairs
Come once and for all into our
Consideration though it be flat like lemonade.
The rest that is dreamed is as the husk
Of this feast on the damp ground.
As I was turning to say something to her she sped by me
Which meant all is over in a few years: twenty-six, twenty-seven,
Who were those people
Who came down to the boat and met us that time?

And your young years become a kind of clay
Out of which the older, more rounded and also brusquer
Retort is fashioned, the greeting
That takes you into night
Like a lantern up ahead:
The "Where *were* you"s; meanwhile
The dark is waiting like so many other things,
Dumbness and voluptuousness among them.
It is good to be part of it
In the dream that is the kernel
Deep in it, the unpretentious, unblushing,
But also the steep side stretching far away:
For this we pay, for this
Tonight and every night.
But for the time being we are free
And meanwhile the songs
Protect us, in a way, and the special climate.

All and Some

And for those who understand:
We shifted that day, until there was no more
Coming out of the situation we had so imitated.
And now we had talked of it
Not as a human being, deeply polite and intelligent
Coming forward to speak things of dark concern
But as a merely interesting description of itself.

Thus all good intentions remain puny
Consigned as they are to the cold dews
And nagging climates of a life's blood.
Does grave dawn drape in a pattern of convolvulus
The next noon alters, dim or baldly untragic
Until the pattern comes to seem no more than footsteps,
Dry and gay, doting on the old-fashioned, the mensual.

"Climate" isn't a sign, but it could be
A by-product, an anonymous blue-collar suburb
In the great mildness that has taken over the air
With snapping cogs, deft reversals.
The blinded sun's got to answer for this
But meanwhile the housing's been built
And actually moved into, some of it.

But what I mean is there's no excuse
For always deducing the general from particulars,
Like spots on that sun. How many
Helpless wails have slid out orchestras
Across skittery dance floors until even
The dancers were there, waltzing lamely at first
But now static and buzzing like plaid? No one

Cares or uses the little station any more.
They are too young to remember
How it was when the late trains came in.
Violet sky grazing the gray hill-crests.
What laziness of appetite
Kept the buzzards circling, and when dawn came
Up it did so on four wheels, without excuses or fuss.

It is impossible to picture the firmness
Of relationships then. The slack
Was by definition taken up, and so
Everything was useful. People died
Delighted with the long wait,
Exhaled brief words into the afternoon, the hills:
Then sweetness was knocked down for the last time.

Do you remember how we used to gather
The woodruff, the woodruff? But all things
Cannot be emblazoned, but surely many
Can, and those few devoted
By a caprice beyond the majesty
Of time's maw live happy useful lives
Unaware that the universe is a vast incubator.

To sense this clearly is not to know it, alas—
Today the directions arrive from many separated realms
Conjoining at the place of a bare pedestal.
Too many armies, too many dreams, and that's
It. Goodbye, you say, until next time
And I build our climate until next time
But the sky frowns, and the work gets completed in a dream.

Oleum Misericordiae

To rub it out, make it less virulent
And a stab too at rearranging
The whole thing from the ground up.
Yes we were waiting just now
Yes we are no longer waiting.

Afterwards when I tell you
It's as though it all only happened
As siding of my story

I beg you to listen
You are already listening

It has shut itself out
And in doing so shut us accidentally in

And meanwhile my story goes well
The first chapter
                    endeth

But the real story, the one
They tell us we shall probably never know
Drifts back in bits and pieces
All of them, it turns out

So lucky
Now we really know
It all happened by chance:
A chance encounter
The dwarf led you to the end of a street
And pointed flapping his arms in two directions
You forgot to misprize him

But after a series of interludes
In furnished rooms (describe wallpaper)
Transient hotels (mention sink and cockroaches)
And spending the night with a beautiful married woman
Whose husband was away in Centerville on business
(Mention this wallpaper: the purest roses
Though the creamiest and how
Her smile lightens the ordeal
Of the last 500 pages
Though you never knew her last name
Only her first: Dorothy)
You got hold of the water of life
Rescued your two wicked brothers Cash and Jethro
Who promptly stole the water of life
After which you got it back, got safely home,
Saved the old man's life
And inherited the kingdom.

But this was a moment
Under the most cheerful sun.
In poorer lands
No one touches the water of life.

It has no taste
And though it refreshes absolutely
It is a cup that must also pass

Until everybody
Gets some advantage, big or little
Some reason for having come
So far
Without dog or woman
So far alone, unasked.

Self-Portrait in a Convex Mirror

As Parmigianino did it, the right hand
Bigger than the head, thrust at the viewer
And swerving easily away, as though to protect
What it advertises. A few leaded panes, old beams,
Fur, pleated muslin, a coral ring run together
In a movement supporting the face, which swims
Toward and away like the hand
Except that it is in repose. It is what is
Sequestered. Vasari says, "Francesco one day set himself
To take his own portrait, looking at himself for that purpose
In a convex mirror, such as is used by barbers...
He accordingly caused a ball of wood to be made
By a turner, and having divided it in half and
Brought it to the size of the mirror, he set himself
With great art to copy all that he saw in the glass,"
Chiefly his reflection, of which the portrait
Is the reflection once removed.
The glass chose to reflect only what he saw
Which was enough for his purpose: his image
Glazed, embalmed, projected at a 180-degree angle.
The time of day or the density of the light
Adhering to the face keeps it
Lively and intact in a recurring wave
Of arrival. The soul establishes itself.
But how far can it swim out through the eyes
And still return safely to its nest? The surface
Of the mirror being convex, the distance increases
Significantly; that is, enough to make the point
That the soul is a captive, treated humanely, kept
In suspension, unable to advance much farther
Than your look as it intercepts the picture.

Pope Clement and his court were "stupefied"
By it, according to Vasari, and promised a commission
That never materialized. The soul has to stay where it is,
Even though restless, hearing raindrops at the pane,
The sighing of autumn leaves thrashed by the wind,
Longing to be free, outside, but it must stay
Posing in this place. It must move
As little as possible. This is what the portrait says.
But there is in that gaze a combination
Of tenderness, amusement and regret, so powerful
In its restraint that one cannot look for long.
The secret is too plain. The pity of it smarts,
Makes hot tears spurt: that the soul is not a soul,
Has no secret, is small, and it fits
Its hollow perfectly: its room, our moment of attention.
That is the tune but there are no words.
The words are only speculation
(From the Latin *speculum*, mirror):
They seek and cannot find the meaning of the music.
We see only postures of the dream,
Riders of the motion that swings the face
Into view under evening skies, with no
False disarray as proof of authenticity.
But it is life englobed.
One would like to stick one's hand
Out of the globe, but its dimension,
What carries it, will not allow it.
No doubt it is this, not the reflex
To hide something, which makes the hand loom large
As it retreats slightly. There is no way
To build it flat like a section of wall:
It must join the segment of a circle,
Roving back to the body of which it seems
So unlikely a part, to fence in and shore up the face

On which the effort of this condition reads
Like a pinpoint of a smile, a spark
Or star one is not sure of having seen
As darkness resumes. A perverse light whose
Imperative of subtlety dooms in advance its
Conceit to light up: unimportant but meant.
Francesco, your hand is big enough
To wreck the sphere, and too big,
One would think, to weave delicate meshes
That only argue its further detention.
(Big, but not coarse, merely on another scale,
Like a dozing whale on the sea bottom
In relation to the tiny, self-important ship
On the surface.) But your eyes proclaim
That everything is surface. The surface is what's there
And nothing can exist except what's there.
There are no recesses in the room, only alcoves,
And the window doesn't matter much, or that
Sliver of window or mirror on the right, even
As a gauge of the weather, which in French is
Le temps, the word for time, and which
Follows a course wherein changes are merely
Features of the whole. The whole is stable within
Instability, a globe like ours, resting
On a pedestal of vacuum, a ping-pong ball
Secure on its jet of water.
And just as there are no words for the surface, that is,
No words to say what it really is, that it is not
Superficial but a visible core, then there is
No way out of the problem of pathos vs. experience.
You will stay on, restive, serene in
Your gesture which is neither embrace nor warning
But which holds something of both in pure
Affirmation that doesn't affirm anything.

The balloon pops, the attention
Turns dully away. Clouds
In the puddle stir up into sawtoothed fragments.
I think of the friends
Who came to see me, of what yesterday
Was like. A peculiar slant
Of memory that intrudes on the dreaming model
In the silence of the studio as he considers
Lifting the pencil to the self-portrait.
How many people came and stayed a certain time,
Uttered light or dark speech that became part of you
Like light behind windblown fog and sand,
Filtered and influenced by it, until no part
Remains that is surely you. Those voices in the dusk
Have told you all and still the tale goes on
In the form of memories deposited in irregular
Clumps of crystals. Whose curved hand controls,
Francesco, the turning seasons and the thoughts
That peel off and fly away at breathless speeds
Like the last stubborn leaves ripped
From wet branches? I see in this only the chaos
Of your round mirror which organizes everything
Around the polestar of your eyes which are empty,
Know nothing, dream but reveal nothing.
I feel the carousel starting slowly
And going faster and faster: desk, papers, books,
Photographs of friends, the window and the trees
Merging in one neutral band that surrounds
Me on all sides, everywhere I look.
And I cannot explain the action of leveling,
Why it should all boil down to one
Uniform substance, a magma of interiors.
My guide in these matters is your self,
Firm, oblique, accepting everything with the same
Wraith of a smile, and as time speeds up so that it is soon

Much later, I can know only the straight way out,
The distance between us. Long ago
The strewn evidence meant something,
The small accidents and pleasures
Of the day as it moved gracelessly on,
A housewife doing chores. Impossible now
To restore those properties in the silver blur that is
The record of what you accomplished by sitting down
"With great art to copy all that you saw in the glass"
So as to perfect and rule out the extraneous
Forever. In the circle of your intentions certain spars
Remain that perpetuate the enchantment of self with self:
Eyebeams, muslin, coral. It doesn't matter
Because these are things as they are today
Before one's shadow ever grew
Out of the field into thoughts of tomorrow.

Tomorrow is easy, but today is uncharted,
Desolate, reluctant as any landscape
To yield what are laws of perspective
After all only to the painter's deep
Mistrust, a weak instrument though
Necessary. Of course some things
Are possible, it knows, but it doesn't know
Which ones. Some day we will try
To do as many things as are possible
And perhaps we shall succeed at a handful
Of them, but this will not have anything
To do with what is promised today, our
Landscape sweeping out from us to disappear
On the horizon. Today enough of a cover burnishes
To keep the supposition of promises together
In one piece of surface, letting one ramble
Back home from them so that these
Even stronger possibilities can remain

Whole without being tested. Actually
The skin of the bubble-chamber's as tough as
Reptile eggs; everything gets "programmed" there
In due course: more keeps getting included
Without adding to the sum, and just as one
Gets accustomed to a noise that
Kept one awake but now no longer does,
So the room contains this flow like an hourglass
Without varying in climate or quality
(Except perhaps to brighten bleakly and almost
Invisibly, in a focus sharpening toward death—more
Of this later). What should be the vacuum of a dream
Becomes continually replete as the source of dreams
Is being tapped so that this one dream
May wax, flourish like a cabbage rose,
Defying sumptuary laws, leaving us
To awake and try to begin living in what
Has now become a slum. Sydney Freedberg in his
Parmigianino says of it: "Realism in this portrait
No longer produces an objective truth, but a *bizarria*....
However its distortion does not create
A feeling of disharmony.... The forms retain
A strong measure of ideal beauty," because
Fed by our dreams, so inconsequential until one day
We notice the hole they left. Now their importance
If not their meaning is plain. They were to nourish
A dream which includes them all, as they are
Finally reversed in the accumulating mirror.
They seemed strange because we couldn't actually see them.
And we realize this only at a point where they lapse
Like a wave breaking on a rock, giving up
Its shape in a gesture which expresses that shape.
The forms retain a strong measure of ideal beauty
As they forage in secret on our idea of distortion.
Why be unhappy with this arrangement, since

Dreams prolong us as they are absorbed?
Something like living occurs, a movement
Out of the dream into its codification.

As I start to forget it
It presents its stereotype again
But it is an unfamiliar stereotype, the face
Riding at anchor, issued from hazards, soon
To accost others, "rather angel than man" (Vasari).
Perhaps an angel looks like everything
We have forgotten, I mean forgotten
Things that don't seem familiar when
We meet them again, lost beyond telling,
Which were ours once. This would be the point
Of invading the privacy of this man who
"Dabbled in alchemy, but whose wish
Here was not to examine the subtleties of art
In a detached, scientific spirit: he wished through them
To impart the sense of novelty and amazement to the spectator"
(Freedberg). Later portraits such as the Uffizi
"Gentleman," the Borghese "Young Prelate" and
The Naples "Antea" issue from Mannerist
Tensions, but here, as Freedberg points out,
The surprise, the tension are in the concept
Rather than its realization.
The consonance of the High Renaissance
Is present, though distorted by the mirror.
What is novel is the extreme care in rendering
The velleities of the rounded reflecting surface
(It is the first mirror portrait),
So that you could be fooled for a moment
Before you realize the reflection
Isn't yours. You feel then like one of those
Hoffmann characters who have been deprived
Of a reflection, except that the whole of me

Is seen to be supplanted by the strict
Otherness of the painter in his
Other room. We have surprised him
At work, but no, he has surprised us
As he works. The picture is almost finished,
The surprise almost over, as when one looks out,
Startled by a snowfall which even now is
Ending in specks and sparkles of snow.
It happened while you were inside, asleep,
And there is no reason why you should have
Been awake for it, except that the day
Is ending and it will be hard for you
To get to sleep tonight, at least until late.

The shadow of the city injects its own
Urgency: Rome where Francesco
Was at work during the Sack: his inventions
Amazed the soldiers who burst in on him;
They decided to spare his life, but he left soon after;
Vienna where the painting is today, where
I saw it with Pierre in the summer of 1959; New York
Where I am now, which is a logarithm
Of other cities. Our landscape
Is alive with filiations, shuttlings;
Business is carried on by look, gesture,
Hearsay. It is another life to the city,
The backing of the looking glass of the
Unidentified but precisely sketched studio. It wants
To siphon off the life of the studio, deflate
Its mapped space to enactments, island it.
That operation has been temporarily stalled
But something new is on the way, a new preciosity
In the wind. Can you stand it,
Francesco? Are you strong enough for it?

This wind brings what it knows not, is
Self-propelled, blind, has no notion
Of itself. It is inertia that once
Acknowledged saps all activity, secret or public:
Whispers of the word that can't be understood
But can be felt, a chill, a blight
Moving outward along the capes and peninsulas
Of your nervures and so to the archipelagoes
And to the bathed, aired secrecy of the open sea.
This is its negative side. Its positive side is
Making you notice life and the stresses
That only seemed to go away, but now,
As this new mode questions, are seen to be
Hastening out of style. If they are to become classics
They must decide which side they are on.
Their reticence has undermined
The urban scenery, made its ambiguities
Look willful and tired, the games of an old man.
What we need now is this unlikely
Challenger pounding on the gates of an amazed
Castle. Your argument, Francesco,
Had begun to grow stale as no answer
Or answers were forthcoming. If it dissolves now
Into dust, that only means its time had come
Some time ago, but look now, and listen:
It may be that another life is stocked there
In recesses no one knew of; that it,
Not we, are the change; that we are in fact it
If we could get back to it, relive some of the way
It looked, turn our faces to the globe as it sets
And still be coming out all right:
Nerves normal, breath normal. Since it is a metaphor
Made to include us, we are a part of it and
Can live in it as in fact we have done,

Only leaving our minds bare for questioning
We now see will not take place at random
But in an orderly way that means to menace
Nobody—the normal way things are done,
Like the concentric growing up of days
Around a life: correctly, if you think about it.

A breeze like the turning of a page
Brings back your face: the moment
Takes such a big bite out of the haze
Of pleasant intuition it comes after.
The locking into place is "death itself,"
As Berg said of a phrase in Mahler's Ninth;
Or, to quote Imogen in *Cymbeline*, "There cannot
Be a pinch in death more sharp than this," for,
Though only exercise or tactic, it carries
The momentum of a conviction that had been building.
Mere forgetfulness cannot remove it
Nor wishing bring it back, as long as it remains
The white precipitate of its dream
In the climate of sighs flung across our world,
A cloth over a birdcage. But it is certain that
What is beautiful seems so only in relation to a specific
Life, experienced or not, channeled into some form
Steeped in the nostalgia of a collective past.
The light sinks today with an enthusiasm
I have known elsewhere, and known why
It seemed meaningful, that others felt this way
Years ago. I go on consulting
This mirror that is no longer mine
For as much brisk vacancy as is to be
My portion this time. And the vase is always full
Because there is only just so much room
And it accommodates everything. The sample
One sees is not to be taken as

Merely that, but as everything as it
May be imagined outside time—not as a gesture
But as all, in the refined, assimilable state.
But what is this universe the porch of
As it veers in and out, back and forth,
Refusing to surround us and still the only
Thing we can see? Love once
Tipped the scales but now is shadowed, invisible,
Though mysteriously present, around somewhere.
But we know it cannot be sandwiched
Between two adjacent moments, that its windings
Lead nowhere except to further tributaries
And that these empty themselves into a vague
Sense of something that can never be known
Even though it seems likely that each of us
Knows what it is and is capable of
Communicating it to the other. But the look
Some wear as a sign makes one want to
Push forward ignoring the apparent
Naïveté of the attempt, not caring
That no one is listening, since the light
Has been lit once and for all in their eyes
And is present, unimpaired, a permanent anomaly,
Awake and silent. On the surface of it
There seems no special reason why that light
Should be focused by love, or why
The city falling with its beautiful suburbs
Into space always less clear, less defined,
Should read as the support of its progress,
The easel upon which the drama unfolded
To its own satisfaction and to the end
Of our dreaming, as we had never imagined
It would end, in worn daylight with the painted
Promise showing through as a gage, a bond.
This nondescript, never-to-be defined daytime is

The secret of where it takes place
And we can no longer return to the various
Conflicting statements gathered, lapses of memory
Of the principal witnesses. All we know
Is that we are a little early, that
Today has that special, lapidary
Todayness that the sunlight reproduces
Faithfully in casting twig-shadows on blithe
Sidewalks. No previous day would have been like this.
I used to think they were all alike,
That the present always looked the same to everybody
But this confusion drains away as one
Is always cresting into one's present.
Yet the "poetic," straw-colored space
Of the long corridor that leads back to the painting,
Its darkening opposite—is this
Some figment of "art," not to be imagined
As real, let alone special? Hasn't it too its lair
In the present we are always escaping from
And falling back into, as the waterwheel of days
Pursues its uneventful, even serene course?
I think it is trying to say it is today
And we must get out of it even as the public
Is pushing through the museum now so as to
Be out by closing time. You can't live there.
The gray glaze of the past attacks all know-how:
Secrets of wash and finish that took a lifetime
To learn and are reduced to the status of
Black-and-white illustrations in a book where colorplates
Are rare. That is, all time
Reduces to no special time. No one
Alludes to the change; to do so might
Involve calling attention to oneself
Which would augment the dread of not getting out

Before having seen the whole collection
(Except for the sculptures in the basement:
They are where they belong).
Our time gets to be veiled, compromised
By the portrait's will to endure. It hints at
Our own, which we were hoping to keep hidden.
We don't need paintings or
Doggerel written by mature poets when
The explosion is so precise, so fine.
Is there any point even in acknowledging
The existence of all that? Does it
Exist? Certainly the leisure to
Indulge stately pastimes doesn't,
Any more. Today has no margins, the event arrives
Flush with its edges, is of the same substance,
Indistinguishable. "Play" is something else;
It exists, in a society specifically
Organized as a demonstration of itself.
There is no other way, and those assholes
Who would confuse everything with their mirror games
Which seem to multiply stakes and possibilities, or
At least confuse issues by means of an investing
Aura that would corrode the architecture
Of the whole in a haze of suppressed mockery,
Are beside the point. They are out of the game,
Which doesn't exist until they are out of it.
It seems like a very hostile universe
But as the principle of each individual thing is
Hostile to, exists at the expense of all the others
As philosophers have often pointed out, at least
This thing, the mute, undivided present,
Has the justification of logic, which
In this instance isn't a bad thing
Or wouldn't be, if the way of telling

Didn't somehow intrude, twisting the end result
Into a caricature of itself. This always
Happens, as in the game where
A whispered phrase passed around the room
Ends up as something completely different.
It is the principle that makes works of art so unlike
What the artist intended. Often he finds
He has omitted the thing he started out to say
In the first place. Seduced by flowers,
Explicit pleasures, he blames himself (though
Secretly satisfied with the result), imagining
He had a say in the matter and exercised
An option of which he was hardly conscious,
Unaware that necessity circumvents such resolutions
So as to create something new
For itself, that there is no other way,
That the history of creation proceeds according to
Stringent laws, and that things
Do get done in this way, but never the things
We set out to accomplish and wanted so desperately
To see come into being. Parmigianino
Must have realized this as he worked at his
Life-obstructing task. One is forced to read
The perfectly plausible accomplishment of a purpose
Into the smooth, perhaps even bland (but so
Enigmatic) finish. Is there anything
To be serious about beyond this otherness
That gets included in the most ordinary
Forms of daily activity, changing everything
Slightly and profoundly, and tearing the matter
Of creation, any creation, not just artistic creation
Out of our hands, to install it on some monstrous, near
Peak, too close to ignore, too far
For one to intervene? This otherness, this
"Not-being-us" is all there is to look at

In the mirror, though no one can say
How it came to be this way. A ship
Flying unknown colors has entered the harbor.
You are allowing extraneous matters
To break up your day, cloud the focus
Of the crystal ball. Its scene drifts away
Like vapor scattered on the wind. The fertile
Thought-associations that until now came
So easily, appear no more, or rarely. Their
Colorings are less intense, washed out
By autumn rains and winds, spoiled, muddied,
Given back to you because they are worthless.
Yet we are such creatures of habit that their
Implications are still around *en permanence*, confusing
Issues. To be serious only about sex
Is perhaps one way, but the sands are hissing
As they approach the beginning of the big slide
Into what happened. This past
Is now here: the painter's
Reflected face, in which we linger, receiving
Dreams and inspirations on an unassigned
Frequency, but the hues have turned metallic,
The curves and edges are not so rich. Each person
Has one big theory to explain the universe
But it doesn't tell the whole story
And in the end it is what is outside him
That matters, to him and especially to us
Who have been given no help whatever
In decoding our own man-size quotient and must rely
On second-hand knowledge. Yet I know
That no one else's taste is going to be
Any help, and might as well be ignored.
Once it seemed so perfect—gloss on the fine
Freckled skin, lips moistened as though about to part
Releasing speech, and the familiar look

Of clothes and furniture that one forgets.
This could have been our paradise: exotic
Refuge within an exhausted world, but that wasn't
In the cards, because it couldn't have been
The point. Aping naturalness may be the first step
Toward achieving an inner calm
But it is the first step only, and often
Remains a frozen gesture of welcome etched
On the air materializing behind it,
A convention. And we have really
No time for these, except to use them
For kindling. The sooner they are burnt up
The better for the roles we have to play.
Therefore I beseech you, withdraw that hand,
Offer it no longer as shield or greeting,
The shield of a greeting, Francesco:
There is room for one bullet in the chamber:
Our looking through the wrong end
Of the telescope as you fall back at a speed
Faster than that of light to flatten ultimately
Among the features of the room, an invitation
Never mailed, the "it was all a dream"
Syndrome, though the "all" tells tersely
Enough how it wasn't. Its existence
Was real, though troubled, and the ache
Of this waking dream can never drown out
The diagram still sketched on the wind,
Chosen, meant for me and materialized
In the disguising radiance of my room.
We have seen the city; it is the gibbous
Mirrored eye of an insect. All things happen
On its balcony and are resumed within,
But the action is the cold, syrupy flow
Of a pageant. One feels too confined,
Sifting the April sunlight for clues,

In the mere stillness of the ease of its
Parameter. The hand holds no chalk
And each part of the whole falls off
And cannot know it knew, except
Here and there, in cold pockets
Of remembrance, whispers out of time.